Beady Eyed Women's Guide to Exquisite Beadwork:
A Peyote Stitch Primer

by Vicki Star and Jeannette Cook
©1994

ISBN Number 1-889789-01-1

Fourth Printing - September, 1996

Written and Illustrated on a Macintosh Color Classic Computer

published by
Beady Eyed Women, Enterprises
P. O. Box 60691
San Diego, CA 92166

Cover Photos: Jeff Tippett

Table of Contents

This Workbook was meant to be <u>used</u>! Scribble notes, make drawings, write down great jokes and Bead Ideas...

Above all - Have a <u>WONDERFUL</u> time!

Pictured on the front cover is a Sculptural Peyote Brooch by *Jeannette Cook.*

Techniques used include: **Basic Flat Peyote** (page 3)
The Curl (page 4)
Ruffle (page 11)

On the back cover, clockwise from top left, are:

Peyote Flowers & variations (page 7) *VS*

Basic Tubular Peyote Crystal top (page 5) *VS*

Peyote Daisy Chain (page 14) *VS*

Ripple Curl Shell (page 4) *JC*

Flat Spiral Kaleidoscope Pendant (page 6) *JC*

Needle Case + Lid (page 6) *JC*

Beaded Bead (page 12) *VS*

Peyote Pouch (page 13) *VS*

Fancy Spiral Tube variation (page 10) *JC*

VS = created by *Vicki Star*   *JC* = created by *Jeannette Cook*

Welcome, Beady Eyed Women!
(And Beady Eyed Men, Too!)

As you may know, beading is an addictive art form. The more techniques you learn and the more beads you buy, the more you want! And why not? You get to create beautiful little sculptures with a never ending array of textures and colors. Beadwork is like miniature stained glass sculptures, but much, much more compact. (I don't know about less expensive, though.)

I first became addicted to beads 26 years ago, and no matter which direction my life has gone, beading has been the constant thread woven throughout all my changes. It has kept me sane during turmoil, helped me remain excited about life when it would have otherwise become mundane, and calmed me when things got too hectic.

I began teaching about 7 years ago at the Shepherdess in San Diego. I stayed there for 3 1/2 years, and then moved on to Oskadusa in Solana Beach, The Black Sheep in Encinitas, Ascona Beads in Santa Monica, DACS Beads in Honolulu, and The Bead Fetish in San Rafael. Now, Vicki and I are holding Beady Eyed Retreats in wonderful locations around the country.

I believe this book will be a useful tool for you. So... sit back, break out your beads, and have fun!

Jeannette Cook

Peyote stitch is one of my favorite techniques because of its rhythm, meditative qualities, simplicity, and unlimited options. You don't need any fancy equipment or advance preparation. All you need is your needle and thread, and your beads, and away you go!!!

I started beading when I was 8 years old in Camp Fire Girls. I learned loom weaving with crow beads, using a cigar box for the loom. I can remember stringing love beads in Junior High School...

In 1985 Marcie Stone at the Shepherdess asked me to teach for her. (Thanks Marcie!) I figured since I had been a Girl Scout Leader and could teach little girls, I could also teach grown women. (They don't fight over the beads quite so much.)

Jeannette and I met while we were teaching. We became bead buddies right off, and have been trading beads and techniques ever since.

I am currently teaching at Oskadusa in Solana Beach, The Black Sheep in Encinitas, Beads 'N' Jewels in Chula Vista, Creative Expressions in Palm Springs, Ascona Beads in Santa Monica, and conducting the Beady Eyed Retreats with Jeannette.

I hope you enjoy this book as much as I enjoyed writing it!

Vicki Star

Ms. Cook's Thread Theory

❖Thread Your Needle

Jeannette uses waxed, doubled and knotted size B Nymo thread and a size 13 needle. (The thread should be about six feet long to start. After you double the thread, you will have three feet with which to work. Leave about four inches between the knot at the end of your thread and the beads.

❖Tieing Off

Weave your needle through 2 or 3 beads just below the last bead your needle passed through. Pick up the thread just outside of the bead where your thread is coming out. Leave a loop, then pass the needle through the loop and tighten into a little knot. Dab a little nail polish or knot glue on the knot. Pass your needle through the bead on the other side of the knot you just made. Cut the thread off.

❖Adding New Thread

Re-thread your needle with a 6 foot piece of thread, double but no knot is necessary. Don't forget to wax your thread! Go through 1 or 2 beads in the area you wish to resume beading. Leaving a tail of thread about 2 to 3 inches long, pick up the thread between the bead you are coming out of and the opposite bead, leave a loop, pass your needle through the loop and tighten into a knot. Glue this knot, then weave your thread through beads until you are at the desired starting point! To find the place where you left off, look for the "three steps down" place on the edge of your beadwork. The rest of the edge will just step up, down, up, down.

Ms. Star's Thread Theory

❖Thread Your Needle

Thread your size 12 needle with 1-1/2 to 2 yards of Nymo B or D thread. (Vicki uses a single strand of thread, like for embroidery.) Wax it, then tie a "stopper" bead loosely on to the end, leaving a 6 to 8 inch tail to weave into the work later. (This bead will be removed before weaving in the tail, so don't count it when counting the first row.)

❖Tieing Off

To tie off, just run the thread through your beads in a zig-zag pattern and cut off the old thread. Try to tie off in the middle of a row (except for the last time!)

You can take off the bead that is tied on, thread the tail through your needle, and tie it off in the same way.

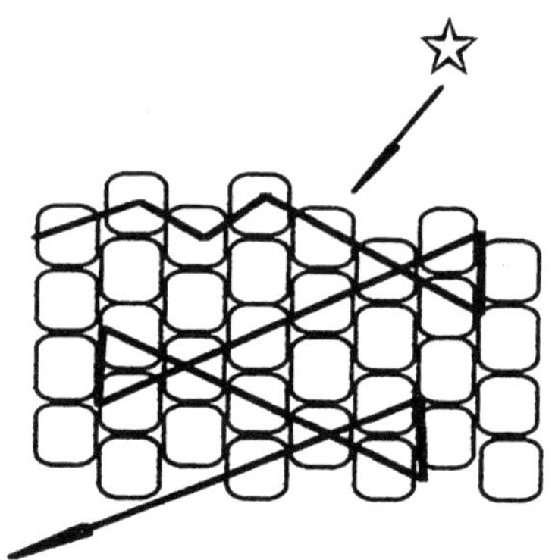

❖Adding New Thread

Thread your needle and wax the thread. (NO KNOTS!) Work the thread zig-zag fashion through some beads to anchor it, and come out where you left off, ready to continue beading. You can find this spot by looking for the place where three beads "stairstep." You want to come out the middle bead, heading towards the lowest "step". (See the star in the drawing.)

Flat Peyote

❖Basic Flat Peyote

[1] Begin with one size and color of seed, hex, or DB. Put an odd number of beads on your thread. (Try 13 to 19 beads to start with). This will result in a strip an even number of beads wide. I. E. start with 13 beads, get a piece 12 beads wide.

[2] Counting from the needle heading for the knot, put your needle through the third bead, marked with a star in the drawing.

Pull the thread all the way through while holding the bead you're passing through with your other hand. The first bead will sit on top of the second bead. (You may need to help it.)

[3] Pick up a bead with your needle and go through the fifth bead, pick up another bead, and go through the seventh bead, continue picking up a bead and going through every other bead to the end of the row.

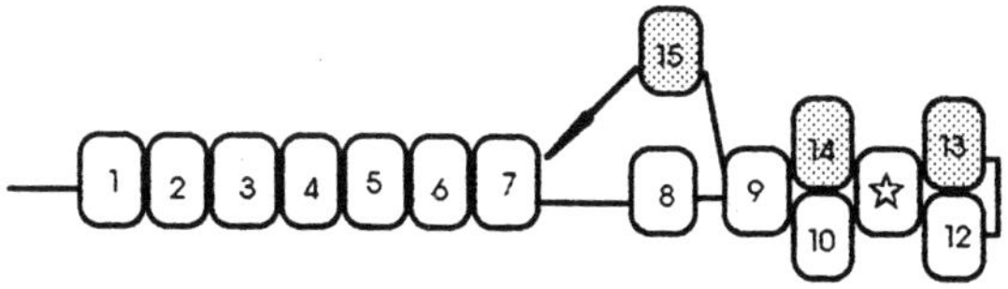

Both the knot and the needle threads will be coming out of the last bead. Tighten your work by taking your finger nails and pushing each set of two beads down away from the knot, then pull the two thread ends apart. (Jeannette says "Tie the threads in three knots, put a dot of clear nail polish or knot glue on the knot you've just tied. Cut the knot thread off." Vicki says "Just keep going. Weave in the tail later!")

[4] Add a bead and go back through the second bead from the end (the "up" bead). Add a bead and go through every other bead ("up" bead) all the way to the end of the row. Repeat until your piece is as tall as you want.

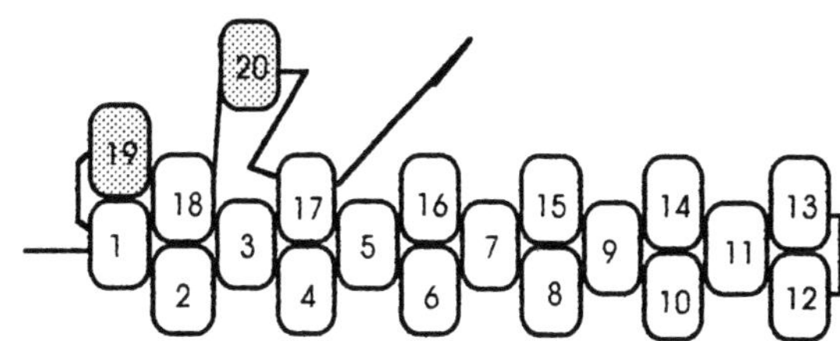

❖Tips:
*Experiment with different colors & sizes of beads to see what will happen.

*Thread up a whole slew of needles before you begin, so you don't have to interrupt your bead rhythm every time you run out of thread.

The Curl

❖Beginning to Curl

[1] When at the end of a row, add two beads instead of one, then turn and go back through the second (or "up") bead.

[2] Add two beads, turn and go back through the bead you just put between the previous two beads.

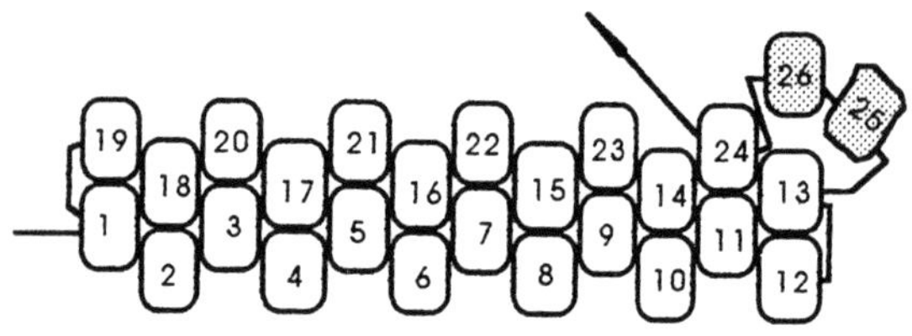

Add one bead between each up bead all the way to the opposite end and back to the "two bead" end.

Continue by adding one bead each time and going through the ("up") bead all the way to the opposite end and back, repeating the step above. The more rows, the bigger the curl!

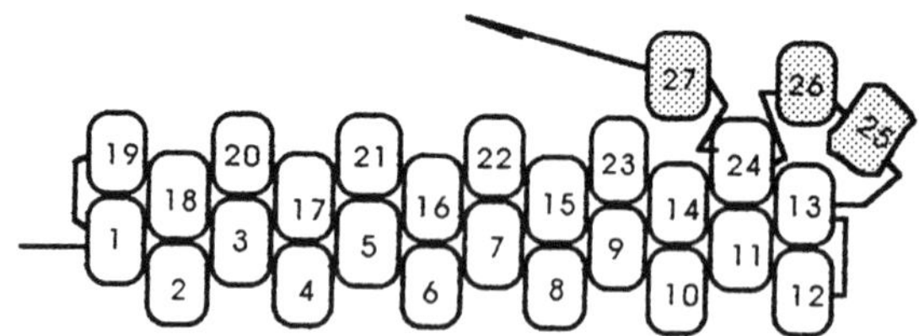

Go through the first of the two beads, add a bead and go through the second of the two beads.

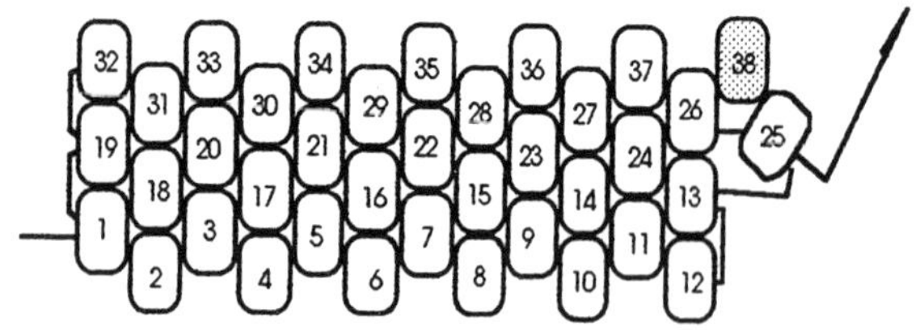

❖Ripple Curl

You will continue the same curl steps, however, vary the size of your beads for 3-6 rows at a time. Increase and decrease the size of your beads, and a ripple will occur in your curl!

To Cover an Object

❖Basic Tubular Peyote

String enough beads to completely encircle your object. Now go through the beads again to make a circle. Tie the tail around the "core" thread if necessary. Don't make this first row too tight - these beads need room to breathe.

Slide the ring onto the item and begin to "peyote". (Working towards the top of the item, begin by *[stringing one bead on your needle, skipping one bead on the "core" thread, and sewing through one bead on the "core" thread]. Repeat from the * until you get all the way around.)

From this point on, you should have an "up" bead to go through. Add one bead to your needle, then sew through the next "up" bead, until the band is as wide as you like.

Continue until the beadwork covers as much area as you desire, increasing and/or decreasing as needed.

❖Totally Tubular Tips

*Be sure to always go in the same direction. (I'm right-handed, so I work from right to left.)

*If a bead is tight the first time your needle goes through it, DON'T use it, since you will have to go through it again, and it might be too tight to fit your thread through a second time.

*Keep your work snug and tight!

Remember . . .

*If you have an <u>even</u> number of beads, be sure to go through <u>TWO</u> beads to begin each row. Each row has a definite beginning and end.

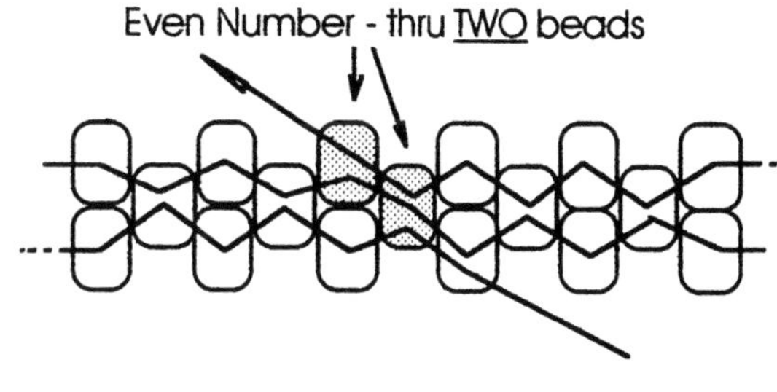

*If there are an <u>odd</u> number of beads, you are actually making one long row that spirals around and around. You will have to pay attention to where each row starts so your pattern will be even. Take this into consideration when planning your design.

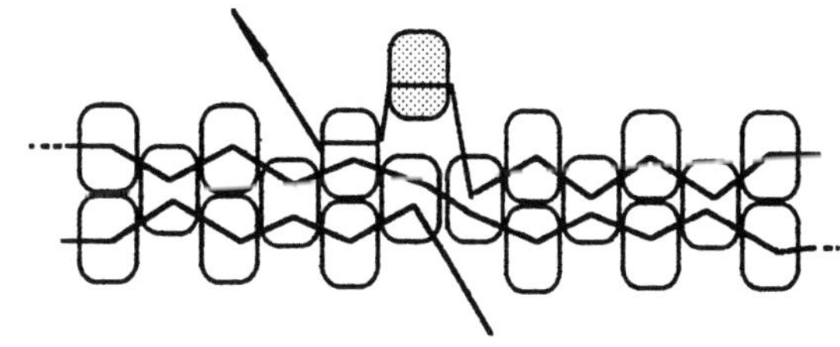

Odd number - just keep going!

Flat Spiral

Basic Flat Spiral

[1] String 3 to 5 beads, then go through them again to make a ring. Be sure to leave a tail to tie off or weave in later.

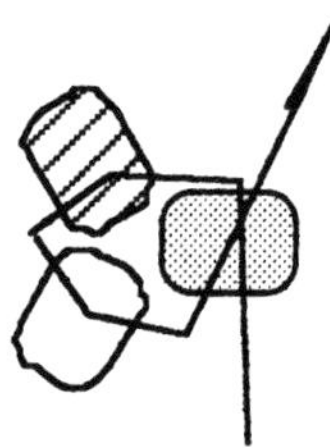

[2] Add 2 beads between each bead of the previous row.

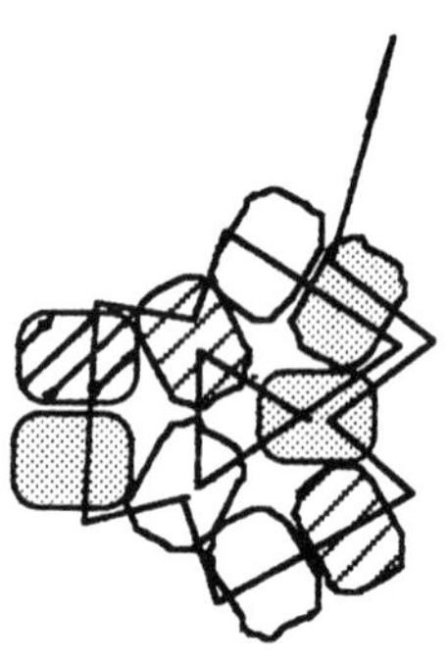

[3] Add 1 bead between each bead of row two.

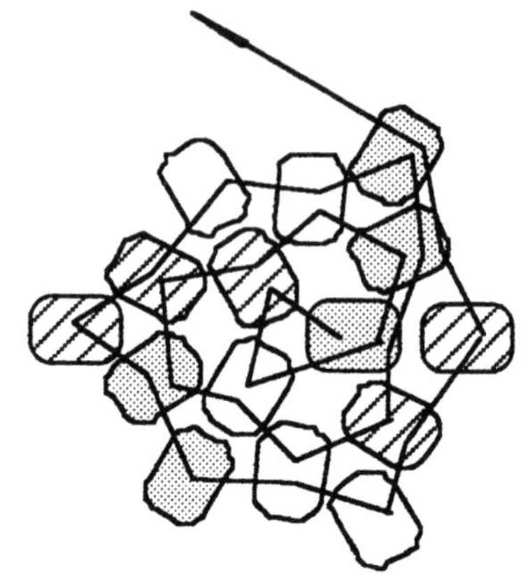

[4] thru Infinity: Continue alternating between increase rows and regular rows, depending on the degree of curve (or flatness) desired, and the sizes of your beads.

❖Tips:

*Finish each row by going through the first bead of the previous row, then the first bead of the current row.

*For a spiral design, make sure the next bead is the same color as the bead you just came out. To reverse the spiral, pick up the same color bead as the bead that you will be going through.

❖Cover Your Needle Case!

Make a flat spiral piece a little bigger than the bottom of your needle case, then stop increasing, but keep on peyote-ing. This will create a tubular peyote case for your case! Do it again for the lid. If you make a zig-zag edge on both pieces, they will fit into each other nicely.

Peyote Flowers

❖ Violet

Begin by threading your #12 needle with size B Nymo. (About 2 <u>feet</u> of thread will be plenty.) Lightly wax your thread. Use a single strand.

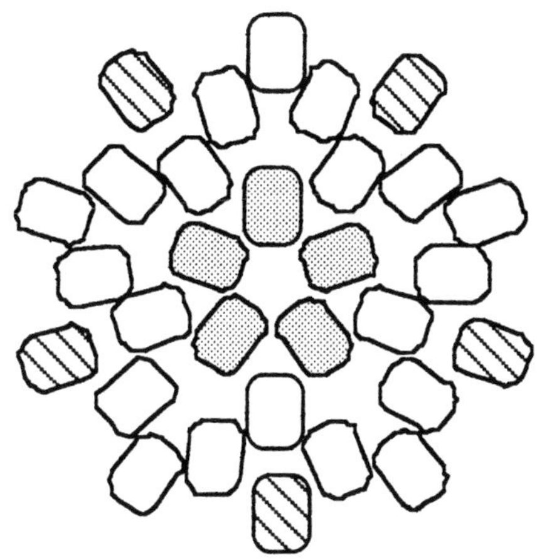

[1] String the beads for your flower center. (**5** yellow for the Violet.) Run your needle through the beads again, in the same direction, to make a ring. Needle through the next bead and pull up tight.

[2] Now begin to "peyote" by adding **1** bead between each bead on the ring. (Add a total of **5** lavender beads.)

[3] Add **2** beads between each "up" bead. (Total of **10** lavender beads.)

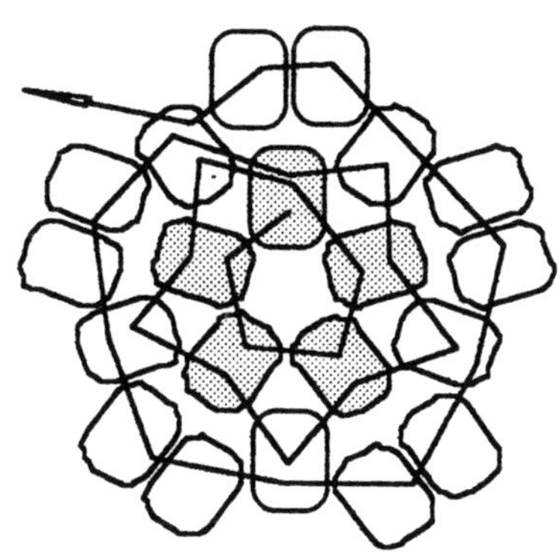

[4] Add **1** bead between each "up" bead. (**1** purple, **1** lavender for a total of **10** beads.)

[5] Add **1** bead between each "up" bead. (Total of **10** purple beads.)

[6] Add **2** purple beads, needle through next **3** purple beads. (Total of **10** purple beads.)

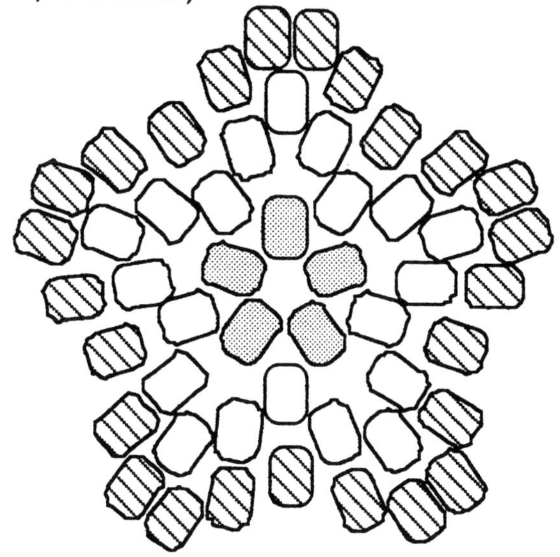

[7] To finish your flower, run your needle through several beads and tie off the "tail". As an option, you can sew a small button or bead to the center of the flower before tieing off.

❖**Tip:** The number of beads in the flower center determines the number of petals. Varying the number of beads added between, and the number of beads the needle goes through at one time, will result in different petal shapes. Experiment and have fun!

Increasing

❖Simple Increasing

Simply use <u>two</u> (skinny) beads in place of one bead where you would like to increase.

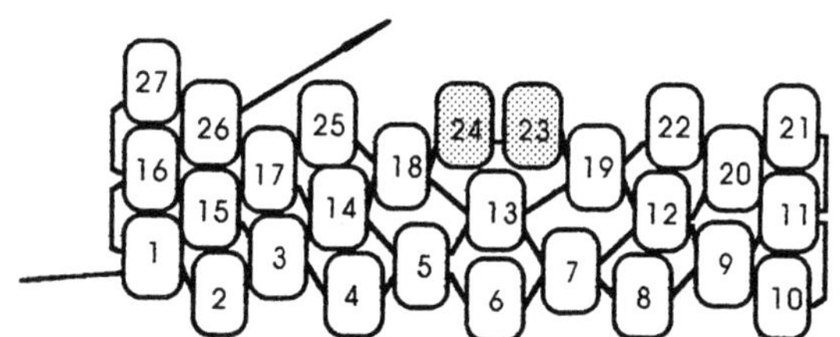

You then add one bead between them in the next row.

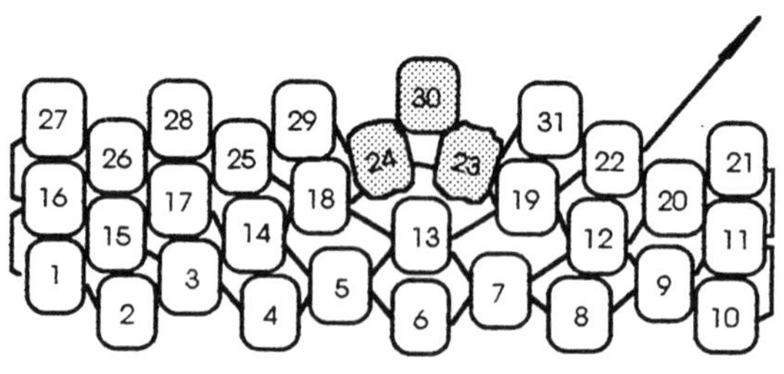

❖Tip:

The drawings are made to show thread between the beads so you can see what's happening. Be sure to keep the tension of <u>your</u> work just right.

❖Double Increase

This method provides a more gradual increase than the one above. Use 2 skinny beads in the spot you want to increase.

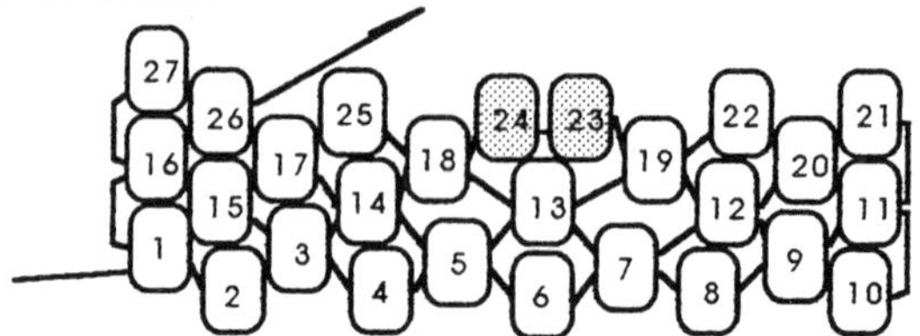

Next time around, needle goes through those two.

Next row, 2 beads same place.

Finally, one bead between those two.

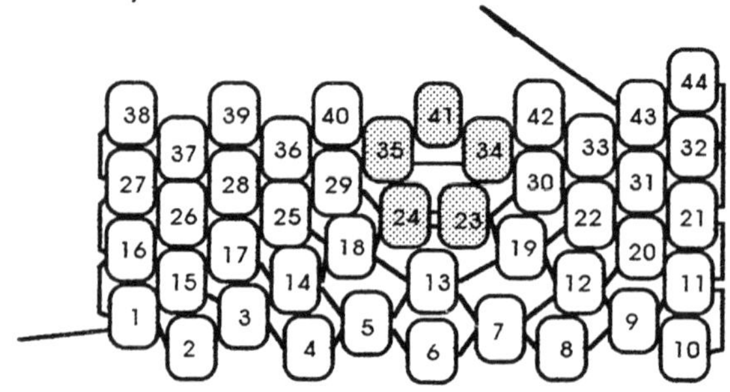

Decreasing

❖Simple Decrease

Wherever you would like to decrease, run your needle through <u>two</u> "up" beads and pull them tightly together.

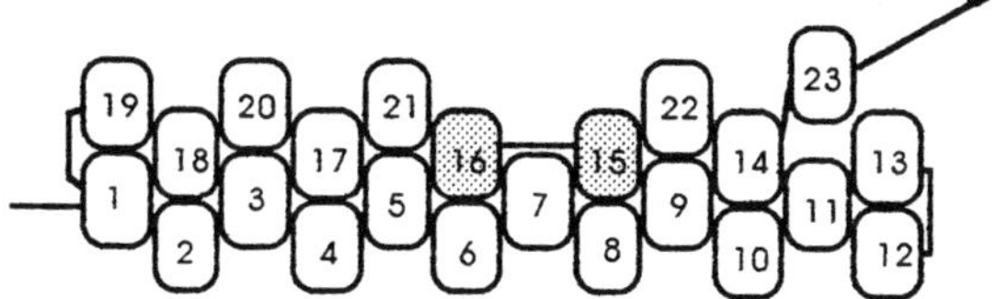

Next row only gets one bead in place of those two.

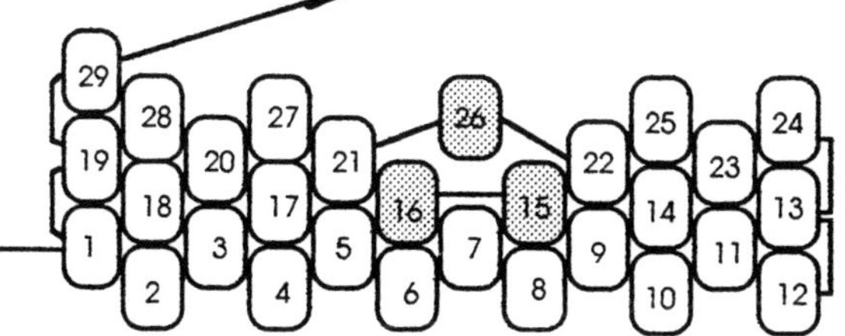

This will decrease the width of your work by two beads.

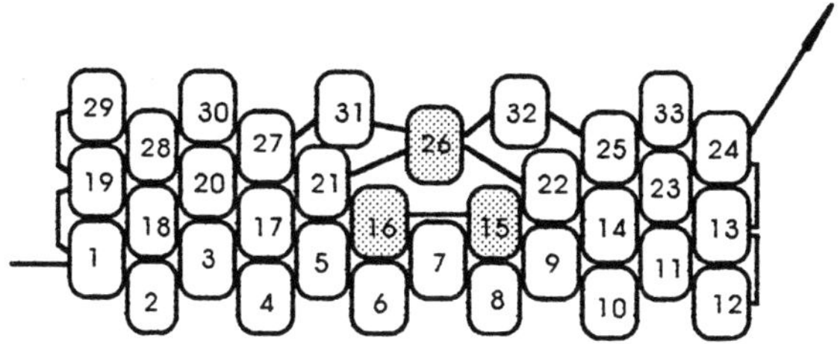

❖Tip:
Remember to pull your beads up nice and snug!

❖Double Decrease

For a more gradual decrease, needle through 2 "up" beads, pull them together.

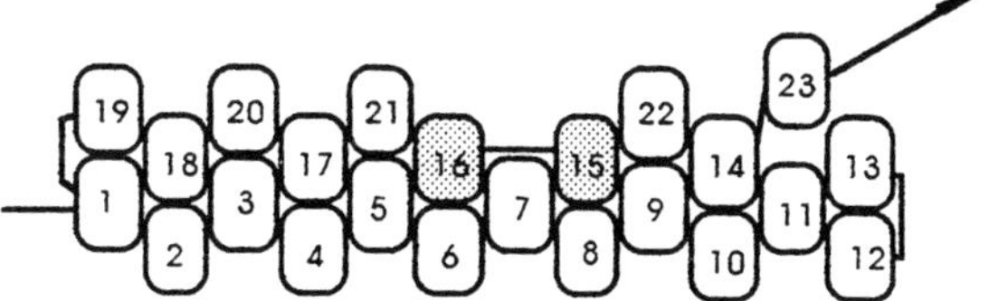

Next row, 2 beads in same spot.

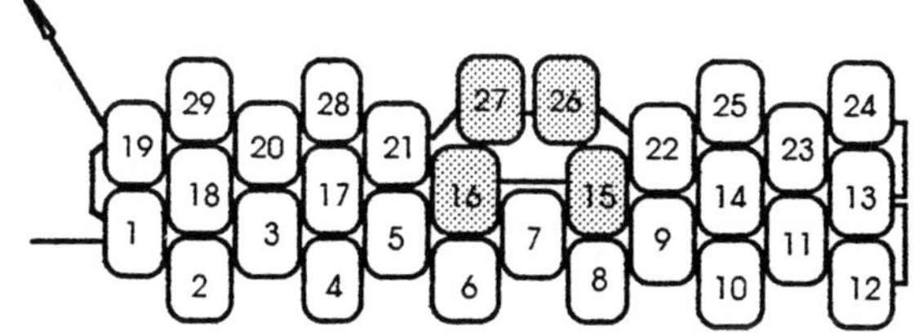

Next time around, needle through those 2 beads.

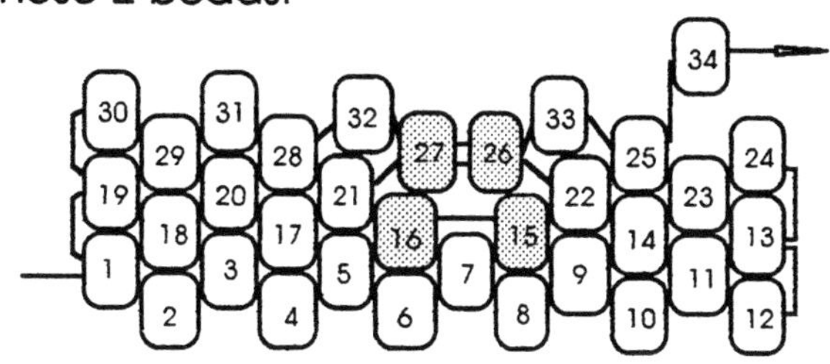

Finally, decrease to 1 bead.

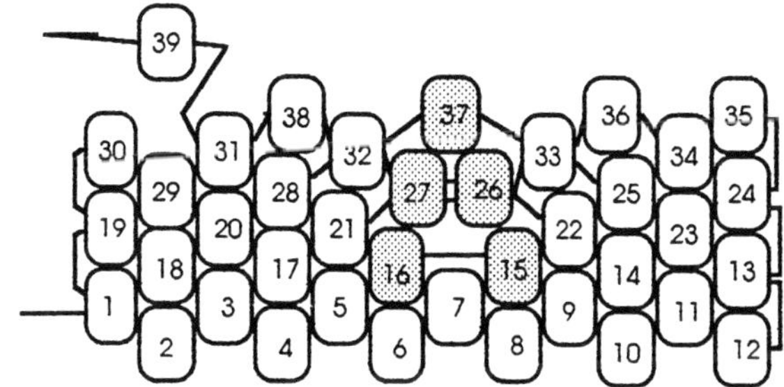

Fancy Spiral Tubes

❖Basic Techique

Vicki says "I got this technique from the Dutch book " Kralen" by Geneke Root. Thanks to Tina McChrie at Oskadusa in Solana Beach for introducing me to this groovy book."

These spirals are a variation on peyote stitched tubes. Designs are created by varying the sizes of your beads, and by using 2 or more beads as a unit (called a "Kralenboogje" or "little bead arch") that takes the place of 1 seed in plain tubular peyote.

For the first round, use two of each bead or unit. (Unless the unit is more than two beads long, then use only one unit.)

On succeeding rows, add the same bead as the one you just came out of. Or, to reverse the spiral, add the same bead that your needle is going in to.

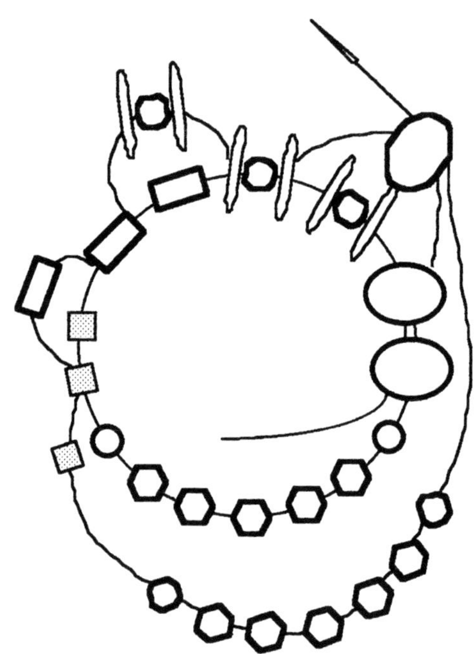

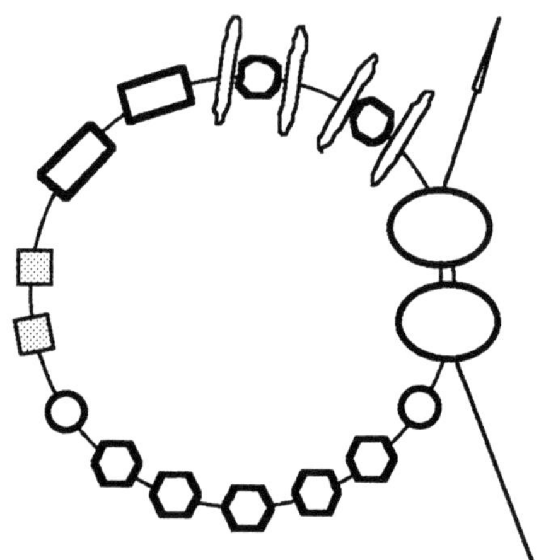

❖Tips:

*The best spirals are rings 7 or fewer beads / units long.

*The more beads in a unit, the lumpier and more snail-like the spiral.

*Make sure that your ring has an odd number of beads / units.

Ruffles and Frills

❖Zig-Zag Edge

*Add one bead, through the next "up" bead, through the next "down" bead, through the next "up" bead, and repeat from *.

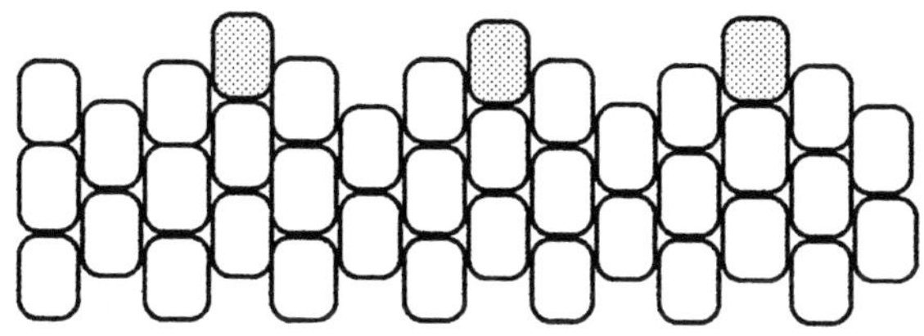

❖Picot or Fleur-de-lis

Wherever you want a little picot on your beadwork, come out a bead, string 3 fleur-de-lis beads; needle through the bead you came out of (in the same direction) to make a circle.

❖Three Bead Netting

Connect 3 beads between each point of the Zig-zag. At the end of each row, run your needle through 3 beads to come out the middle bead. Connect each web to the 2nd (middle) bead of the 3 you added on the previous row.

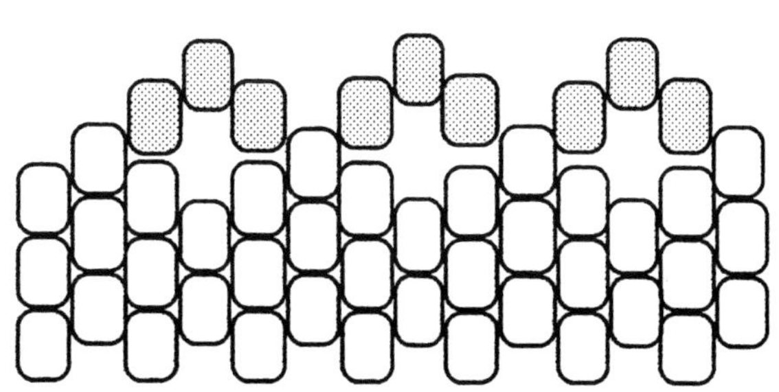

❖Ruffle

Increase the number of beads in each row of netting. (I. E. 3, then 5, 7, etc.) This is also known as the Ogalala Butterfly.

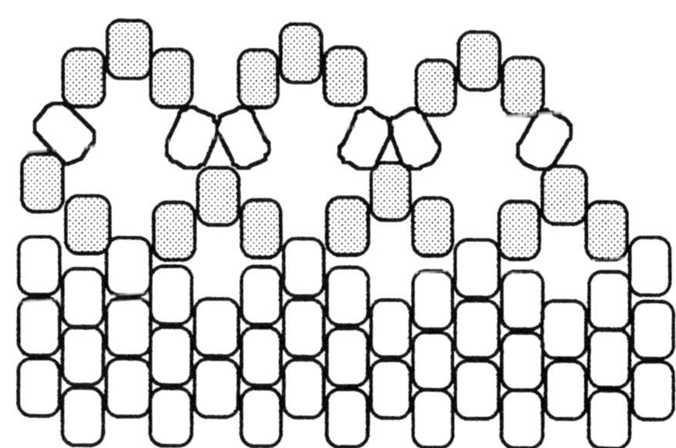

Peyote Beads

❖Easy Bead

Simply make a flat peyote square or rectangle and sew up the edges (like a zipper) to create a tubular peyote "bead"! Vary the bead sizes for wavy beads.

❖Popover Bead

Make a flat peyote square, then fold two opposite corners together and connect them with a few stitches.

Variation: Fold all four corners together and secure them with thread and/or beads.

❖Beaded Bead

String enough seeds to encircle the midline of your Master Bead. Tie the tail to make a ring. Anchor this ring by going through the hole of your master bead, then through a seed. Do this 5 or 6 times at equal distances around the ring.

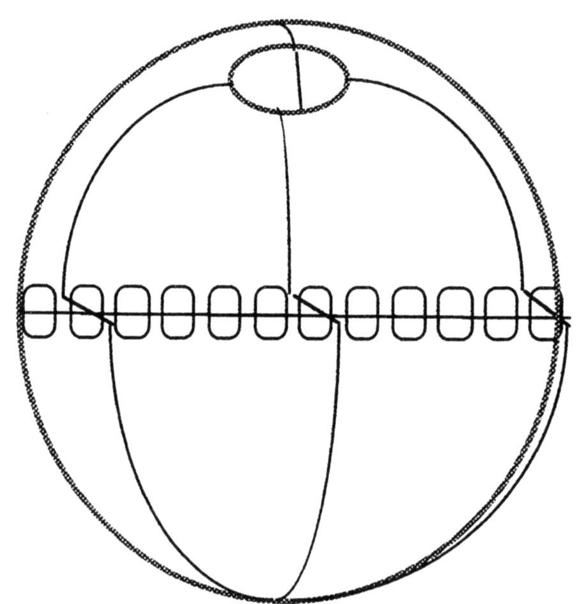

Work a few rows of peyote in one direction, then weave through the band and work in the other direction for a few more rows. Work back and forth, decreasing as you go. Use double or single decreasing according to the shape of the Master Bead and the size of your seeds.

Peyote Pouch

This pouch is started on the bottom "seam", then worked in a spiral fashion till it is as tall as you like.

Start your pouch by stringing on an even number of beads to equal the width of your pouch. Add one bead and go through the previous bead (towards the tail).

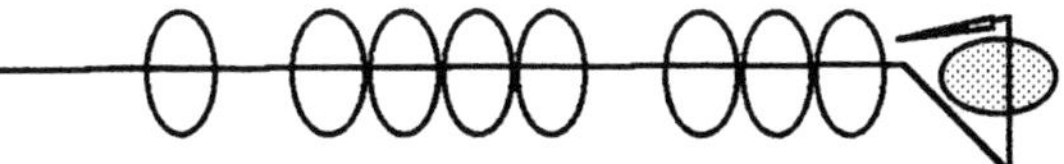

Add one bead, skip one bead in your first row, and go through the next. Repeat all the way to the end. (This completes the first 3 rows!) You should have one bead on the tail thread and one bead on your needle thread.

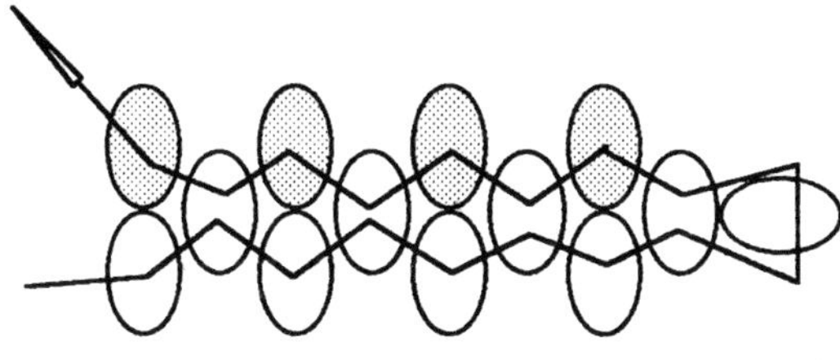

Put the needle through the lall bead (the very first bead you put on your thread) pointing toward the second bead.

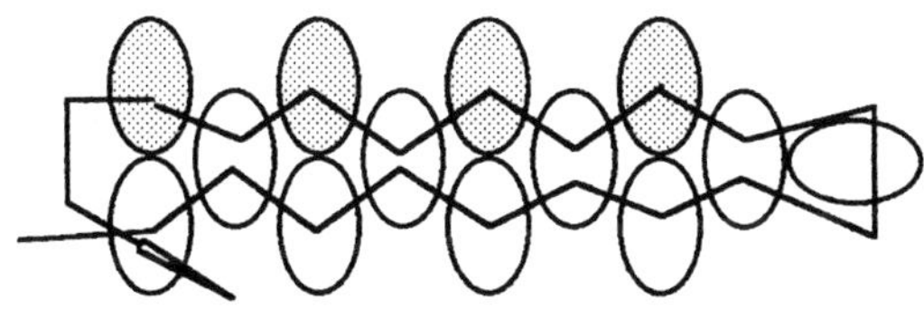

Now, continue adding one bead between each up bead, spiraling towards the top of the pouch, until it is as tall as you want.

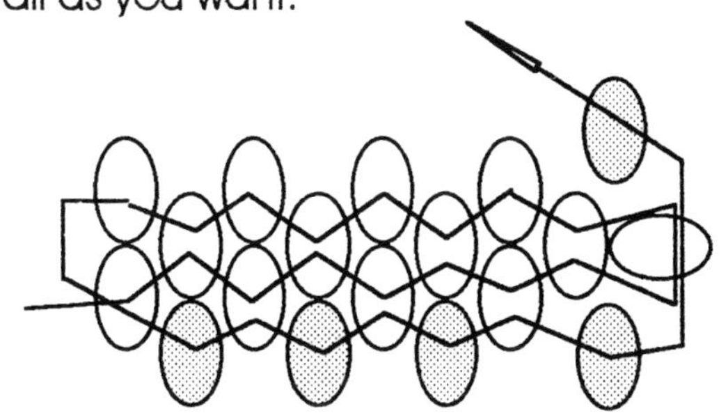

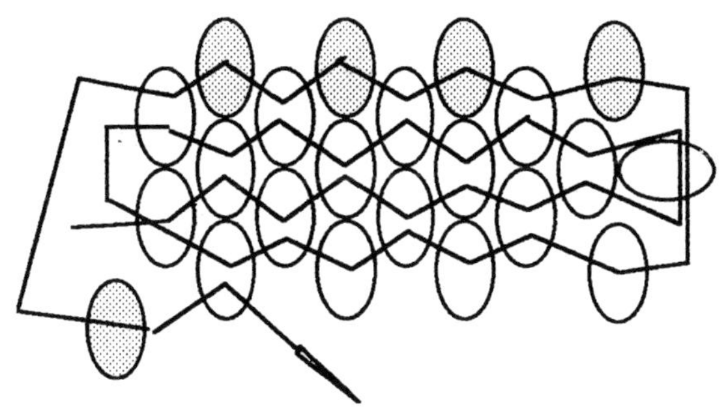

You will notice that one side "seam" has thread showing, while the other side "seam" has a bead on the edge. Each time you get to the thread seam, it is the end of one row.

To make a flap, turn the pouch over for the next row, instead of going around, and work back and forth, Flat Peyote style, until the flap is long enough to fold over the top and down as far as you like.

Peyote Daisy Chain

Make a peyote strip just 4 beads wide. Put the beads on in the following order: 2 background color beads, 2 petal color beads, 1 center color bead, needle back thru 2nd petal bead from needle.

This chain makes a great choker or bracelet, or a terrific strap on an amulet pouch.

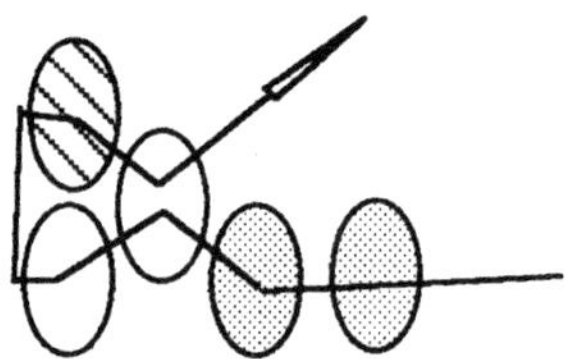

Follow the color chart below, and, at the appropriate spot, add the 3 outside petal beads.

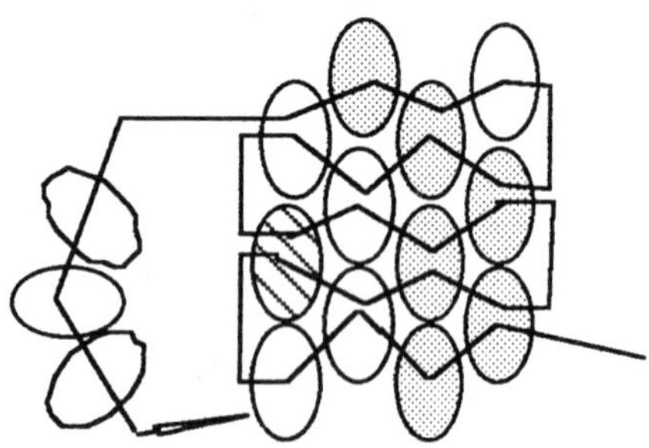

Run your needle thru the petal beads in the chain and then continue to peyote.

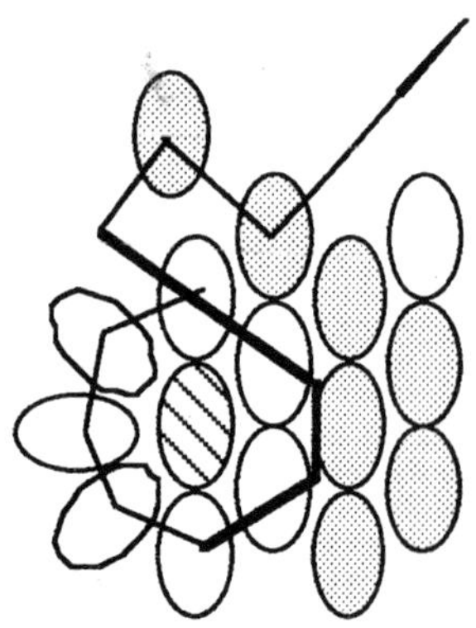

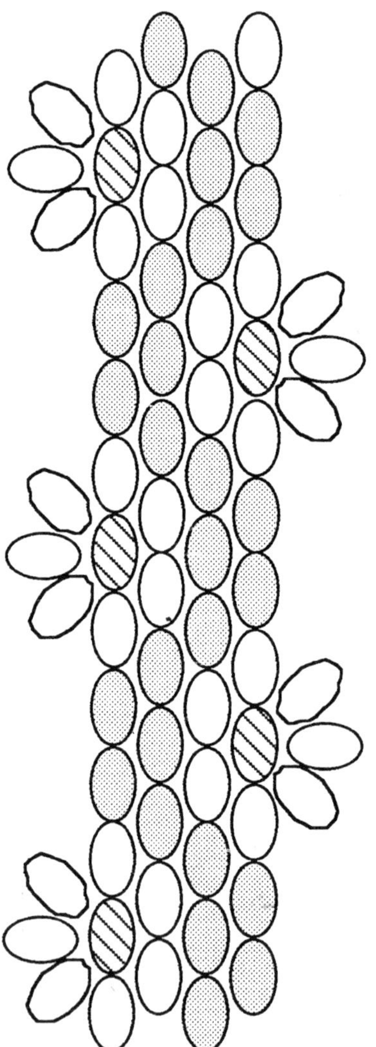

Take this page to your favorite copy store. Have them make you a transparency. Lay
the transparency on top of the picture you want to chart, then make another copy. . .
Viola! You have a charted graph!

You can also reduce or enlarge this page according to your bead size.

Your notes and drawings:

<u>Bead Happy!</u>

Your notes and drawings:

Bead Happy!